Number Two

Number Two

Joshua L. Light

FOREWORD BY
Clint Blevins

RESOURCE *Publications* · Eugene, Oregon

NUMBER TWO

Resource Publications
An Imprint of Wipf and Stock Publishers
199 W. 8th Ave., Suite 3
Eugene, OR 97401

www.wipfandstock.com

PAPERBACK ISBN: 978-1-6667-4533-7
HARDCOVER ISBN: 978-1-6667-4534-4
EBOOK ISBN: 978-1-6667-4535-1

06/28/22

Contents

Foreword

HAVE YOU EVER WONDERED what it would be like to adorn camel skin, offer crunchy treats of wild honey and locust, while all the time redirecting the focus to raise up someone else? Do you dream of how to make yourself less noticeable and others more noticeable? Have you ever longed to be alive but also a sacrifice? Well, in point of fact, these are not my first thoughts in the morning. It's not the common action of mankind to discover new and fascinating ways to die to ourselves, but that is the challenge that Joshua Light has put forth in his book, *Number Two*.

In a world full of "likes" and "posts" it truly is difficult to imagine how the apostle Paul got the word out without the internet, "Without which no man will see the sermon" (Urban Bible . . . maybe). Yet, the message has never changed in all these years. I can't stress how many times I've heard people ask how can the church thrive in the twenty-first century? No one asks, "How do I eat food or love my parents in the twenty-first century?" They simply do it. How do you love God in the modern age? "By loving Him and doing what he commands."

In this book, Josh takes us on a journey that I hope is as humorous to you as much as it is encouraging. *Number Two* is a subtle reminder that the commission remains intact. We're still supposed to put others above ourselves. Basically, to go forth and make disciples. Not disciples of us but of the Lord Jesus Christ. Want to know the difference? Well, I'll let Josh explain.

Oh, and his official title is Keeper of the Golden Arches and Protector of Batman Pinball. We will address him as such.

—**Clint Blevins**, CIO and Global Developer at Reformed
Evangelistic Fellowship

Acknowledgments

With sincere thanksgiving to our living God for their wise counsel, their contagious love of Jesus Christ, their corrections, their laughter, their smiles, and their patience as defined in I Corinthians 13, this book is dedicated to

Dr. Rick J. and Mrs. Evangeline W. Light, Dr. Jim and Mrs. Linda Richter, Dr. Harry and Mrs. Cindy Reeder, Dr. Allen M. III, and Mrs. Wini Baker

Family and friends:

JB, JH, CH, R and RP, A and TE, HR, TS, HS, SB, PB, CB, NB, CB, NL, VLR, JR, BL, BW, MRW, OVL, BLR, JEL, TJ, JM, BW, CF, J and MB, M and JB, JS, GS, BH, DA, A and AD, D and MB, KS, JH, AM

As well as the congregations and leaders of

Cornerstone PCA (Mission Church), Conyers, GA (1983-1985)

Horse Creek Freewill Baptist Church, Kingsport, TN (1985-1987)

Eastern Heights Presbyterian, Bristol, TN (1987-present)

Briarwood PCA, Birmingham, AL (2009-2012)

Evangel Church PCA, Alabaster, AL (2009-2012)

Westminster PCA, Johnson City, TN (2015-2019)

These are among the valued individuals whom I've had the privilege of calling family and friends, mentors, and companions:

"partner[s] in the Gospel from the first day until now." For each of you, I will be eternally grateful, and I firmly believe that your crowns in glory will be in abundance for putting up with me.

Introduction

ALLOW ME TO EXPRESS my sincere thankfulness to you, the reader of this eleven-week devotional. The heart behind the book is light-hearted, and I wrote it to encourage you to become involved in your local Bible-believing, God-fearing, Bible-teaching church or in general service to your community. It's easy to become frustrated when you are committed to serving God (as a pastor, how well I know!), and with that in mind, this devotional will, Lord willing, be used not just for a good laugh, but for a serious examination of how you are serving our Heavenly Father. It is my sincere prayer that the Lord will continue to grow His church in the midst of these troubling years, and will use all of His children to accomplish the work intended for us as His servants laboring in the kingdom here on earth.

This devotional is intended for a small group study and is best accomplished in the space of eleven weeks. Within each of the chapters are a few thought-provoking questions which are geared toward beginning the conversation, and are in no way an exhaustive list of questions—I'm certain many more could be added. Although a little homework is required with some of the studies, it's well worth taking the time to examine yourselves so you will be better prepared and encouraged to either begin your service to our Lord Jesus, or continue in your service for His glory with a renewed mind and heart.

All Scripture references are to the English Standard Version. Enjoy!

—Rev. Joshua Light

Chapter 1: So Long as It Depends on You

I COULD GO OFF down a cynical road of clever phrases and stories, and really talk you out of studying this, but I'm not going to do that . . . at least not too much. This book is all about serving others in the name of Christ, and I'm going to start with the best living examples I know, my parents. They get what it means to be a servant, and I don't say that just to appease the Fifth Commandment. My dad and my former pastors love their families, the church, their work, and sincerely do all things for the glory of God. People love them. People continually take advantage of their hearts and willingness to serve, and, specifically with my father, as his oldest son, it really pushes my buttons. But he, like my pastors, knows his reward is not yet, but coming. These wise counselors constantly urge me to remember that in my affairs. My dad and my mother, Evangeline Wilkinson Light, have been my lifelong teachers of the Word. Boy, were there times when they had every right in the world to end my life and then sing the hymn (slightly revised), "Take [his] life and let it be . . . over," but they remained *faithful*. They are the best No. 2s I know, and I love my parents dearly. I'll hunt down anyone who messes with my mentors, and I'm nowhere near as nice as they are, so be warned. To them and their brides, know that I am grateful for y'all every day.

No one alive or red-blooded wants to be No. 2. We immediately associate that phrase with, umm, other things too, don't we? It's synonymous with a particular movement of the body for a reason. But let me tell you why it's the perfect place, and why the church is in survival recruitment mode because of our type.

No one wants to be second, 'cause you don't get the final say. In East Tennessee where I live, we say, "It ain't up to you!" Congratulations! You get to be the person that others don't have a clue what to do with. If you're like me, I tinkered around in undergrad long enough to know I didn't have a clue what I wanted to do with my life and thought, well, maybe ministry. Trust me when I say that pursuing the ministry is a bit more complex than that, but after 304 credit hours of college, I've learned a simple response to give when people ask why I know I'm called to the ministry: "God won't let me do anything else." He's not mean; He's jealous. He knows what makes me tick, and through sanctification, He knows exactly how I can tick best for Him. Here's another glorious Southern phrase that makes the point— "Son, you ain't goin' anywhere, so ya might as well take your shoes off and make yourself at home."

But let me back up for a minute and introduce myself properly. Hello, ☺ my name is Joshua Light, and so far in my life God has allowed me to serve him in a bunch of really awesome ways. I've been an assistant pastor, adjunct professor, international missionary, professional student, COO, business manager, pulpit supply, and self-taught tech professional. I'm also a son, a brother, and an uncle and as of this writing, I'm thirty-eight. I am guessing there are those of you in the North who are reading this, and you probably have ideas about my accent. You're right, but I guarantee you my voice is deeper and cooler-sounding than yours.

I used to do a few radio spots, I talk a lot (which is a testimony in itself), and people still think I'm Barry White or my father on the phone . . . his voice is even deeper than mine. We sound pretty awesome. I'll tell you my side of the story later, but I'll say here the deep voice that no longer stammers and stutters is of the Lord, and I've got to use it for his glory, no matter what I do because it's a specific answer to a specific prayer.

Let me remind you what this book is about: servanthood.

No one in ministry wants to be No. 2—shoot, no one in life wants to be a No. 2 either. I've been privileged to be in the church for a long time. Truth is, I spent way too many years in school—I aced the biblical languages courses, theology, and all the other-ologies, and had some really solid professors I'm still friends with, but I didn't pay enough attention to the practical part, I guess. Being part of that family of believers has its ups and downs.

Along with the many of blessings of being part of a church family, there are times it can also be hurtful. Let me start my No. 2 discussion in a place you might think unlikely: technology. These days, it is automatically assumed that anyone my age is completely able to do anything technology-related. Having been in a multitude of differing ministries, I've found this assumption has led to some frustrations that all people my age experience from time to time. For example, I must have not known about the course "Technology and Ministry 101"—your ordination depends on whether or not you can fix computer problems you know (sarcasm) . . . It's so bad now that when the coffee maker quits working, I say, "Well, the internet's out again. Gotta' have internet to make coffee." Maybe I should call this book "Rants of a Seminarian Who Didn't Pay Attention" . . . nah . . . I like No. 2. I still love my church family, even if they think I invented the internet, which I didn't. That was Al Gore. He also invented supernovas.

"Email won't work!" "The swoosher isn't swooshing!" (When you send email through Mac's mail program, it makes a swoosh sound. When I was on staff at a church, we made T-shirts for the office staff with the phrase "The swoosher isn't swooshing!" We were all nuts in a good way.) "Can you make a CD for me?" "Why won't our projector turn on?" "Can you sit on the phone and wait on the cable people for us?" "Why won't this printer work?" "My computer don't turn on!" "I'm freezin'!" Fill in your common questions or phrases here. And to top it all off is when the higher ups walk in and say something to the effect of, "You're not doing enough!" Now maybe your situation is different, but the point is, you were yelled at or criticized, and your flesh (like mine) wants to lash out and put that meanie in their place. But *stop!* Remember who your true Boss is. Let him handle the complainers.

A good example of keeping cool in the face of criticism is Arnold Palmer. I enjoy playing golf myself and always admired how Arnold Palmer handled himself. He walked into the clubhouse at Augusta for the first time and was greeted by two elites of the day. They looked this young man up and down in non-sponsored attire and asked him the following: "How in the [world] did they let you in this tournament?" Arnold's response is something all No. 2s everywhere need to nail down immediately if we're going to make it. Arnold looked at the interviewer, who was asking him about this event, and said with an experienced smile, "I didn't say the natural thing . . . I wanted to!"

Here's my point. Don't just react when times of frustration happen. Consider that the men and women who have been serving for longer than you've been alive are tired, and frankly, some are plum wore out. Could be your teacher, pastor, employer, board chairman—you name it. They need you to help them, and sometimes the only way they can express it is by showing that occasional display of exasperation. This is what we need to re-member. Every. Single. Time. It's also how, maybe one day, we can reflect on situations like that and change them . . . maybe. Love on our leaders even more, and help them out to the best of our ability, for the glory of God.

Okay, time to get serious. As I said, this book is about No. 2, a place on the ladder where no one wants to be. But Romans 12—the book we're going to be looking at here—has a lot to say about the importance and value of being second.

Yes, there are other places in the Bible that talk about servant-hood, but Romans 12 is comprehensive and starts with an urgent call: "I appeal . . ." And what and to whom is the appeal? Read on.

> . . . to you therefore, brothers, by the mercies of God, to present your bodies as a living sacrifice, holy and ac-ceptable to God, which is your spiritual worship. Do not be conformed to this world, but be transformed by the renewal of your mind, that by testing you may discern what is the will of God, what is good and acceptable and perfect. For by the grace given to me I say to everyone among *you not to think of himself more highly than he ought to think*, but to think with sober judgment, each according to the measure of faith that God has assigned.

Do you get what the Apostle Paul is saying here? I've put it in italics for emphasis. Don't miss it! The teaching is central to our attitude and actions as Christians, because it models how our Lord performed his ministry with perfect humility. It is one of his awesome attributes.

> For as in one body we have many members, and the members do not all have the same function, so we, though many, are one body in Christ, and individually members one of another. Having gifts that differ according to the grace given to us, let us use them: if prophecy, in proportion to our faith; if service, in our serving; the one who teaches, in his teaching; the one who exhorts, in his exhortation; the one who contributes, in generosity; the one who leads, with zeal; the one who does acts of mercy, with cheerfulness. Let love be genuine. Abhor what is evil; hold fast to what is good. Love one another with brotherly affection. Outdo one another in showing honor. Do not be slothful in zeal, be fervent in spirit, serve the Lord. Rejoice in hope, be patient in tribulation, be constant in prayer. Contribute to the needs of the saints and seek to show hospitality.

Paul then goes on to advise us to do the opposite of what comes naturally:

> Bless those who persecute you; bless and do not curse them. Rejoice with those who rejoice, weep with those who weep. Live in harmony with one another. Do not be haughty, but associate with the lowly. Never be wise in your own sight. Repay no one evil for evil, but give thought to do what is honorable in the sight of all. If possible, so far as it depends on you, live peaceably with all. Beloved, never avenge yourselves, but leave it to the wrath of God, for it is written, 'Vengeance is mine, I will repay, says the Lord.'" To the contrary, "if your enemy is hungry, feed him; if he is thirsty, give him something to drink; for by so doing you will heap burning coals on his head. Do not be overcome by evil, but overcome evil with good.

Let's return to Paul's opening phrase, "I appeal," as he addresses the church in Rome. Allow me to don my old and dusty Greek cap for a moment: the original language shows us that the meaning of this phrase is a *pleading*, or one who is making a case so that the listener/receiver will be behooved to act in the suggested way. Paul is saying here in layman's terms, I beg you, or I urge you. It's much the same as a friend urging you to go with them to a movie when you really don't want to, or someone (or yourself) imploring you not to eat the second Big Mac or Whopper. Paul's urgent appeal is for all of us, so we'd better pay attention and get this right, or we're going to blow it.

The apostle goes on to discuss some key areas of service for the Christian. It is summed up to say that each of us has a specific assignment. Yes, many times we'll be asked either to help someone with something or do it for them. Central to the entire chapter is a phrase in verse 18: ". . . so far as it depends on you," and guess what? Yep, that's us. That's the responsibility of the No. 2. Peace comes as a result of the No. 2s taking care of the matters that disrupt the peace of our fellow man. We'll dive deeper into this later on in the book.

Assistant, associate, co-laborer, non-boss, employee, son/daughter, person with red blood, and/or anyone who drinks water and breathes air—this book is for you. Don't let being a servant drive you mad 'cause it will very quickly. You'll burn out. So, let's talk about it.

Study Questions

1. What's your story? Take some time here and explain who you are and how God has brought you to this point in your life.

2. When you think of being a servant, what comes to mind?

3. If being teachable and humble are desirable qualities in a Christian, are you growing in those areas and if so, how? If no, what might you do to change that?

4. Write out your schedule and ask, am I allowing myself time to serve the Lord and his church?

Personal Reflection(s)

Chapter 2: Everybody! Church Is Cancelled Tonight! The Internet Isn't Working!

IF YOU DIDN'T BURN the book after reading the first chapter, love your heart. So glad you're here to stay! Clearly you're turning out to be a cool No. 2. So, let's get down to it.

I suspect you're asking, what's up with this chapter title? As a former assistant pastor serving at a church in Johnson City, Tennessee (the name will remain anonymous to protect the innocent), I can tell you the chapter title is far closer to being true not only in the church setting but in several other settings where tech help is needed. It's meant to be humorous but may also give rise to a serious moan within you. As a newfound expert in any and all things tech-related (I call myself an expert because, convenient as it is, the majority of the time when help is needed no one else knows how to use the technology or was available to learn— please pick up my cynicism here, dear reader)— again as a tech expert, let me explain what I mean by the chapter title.

The internet pretty much drives our world, and sadly (for reasons I'll soon explain), it's becoming more and more prominent in the church too. Think of all it does for your place of business, your church, your home, your office, the coffee machine, your dog— yeah, most things run on internet. At the church where I oversaw the technology, the office phones are now internet-based and have a wide range of cyberspace necessities. As a result, these require what is known as monitoring and maintenance (insert SpongeBob "Imagination" hand rainbow reveal here—YouTube that clip and insert "monitoring and maintenance" in place of imagination, then you'll hear what's in my head when you're reading this). You can bet that behind your sound system, PowerPoint/Keynote, anything tech-related, there's a No. 2 at the controls. Faithful, unnoticed, under-appreciated, and yet, there they are. Be sure to thank your techies. I can tell you from experience that a simple thank you means the world. They'll go through fire with you gladly if you love on 'em just a little. Pat them on the head. Take them to eat even if their diet is weird. Invite them to your home and have conversation. Anyone can assist! The service opportunities for helping with tech needs are ever growing.

Technology may be vital in church and ministry, but we gotta be careful not to let it replace one-on-one relationships. For me, the model is my alma mater, Birmingham Theological Seminary, and the heart it has for people. We were put in multi-denominational pulpits and on the streets. We shared the gospel door-to-door, and we visited people—we talked to them, we listened, we loved. My seminary wasn't an elitist venue where we sat around and conversed over our latest findings on Calvin, Luther, Spurgeon, and those church leaders past and present who royally blew it—in our expert opinions, of course. In other words, we put our faith and knowledge into practice. Thank God we didn't have Bill Gates show up and give us the latest Microsoft seminar, or have to accommodate Tim Cook on a flyover from Cupertino to show us a keynote. We wrote papers, and then we put flesh on them. And yet somehow, we made it through seminary.

A verse from 2 John 12 relates this concept powerfully: "Though I have much to write to you, I would rather not use paper and ink. Instead, I hope to come to you and talk face to face, so that our joy may be complete." It's kind of fun to imagine what John the Revelator would have tweeted if he'd had access to social media like we do. Maybe, "Guys, there is so much I gotta tell ya, so we have to meet up soon! #epic #letsgettogetheryeahyeahyeah" (English translation).

Allow me to do some pastoral application work on the short chapter in 2 John where we find that verse, and I'll bring in other Scriptures as well to show the idea. John is thrilled that some of the children are walking down the right paths (also reference Jer 6:16), and then as we read 2 John 12, we come to the understanding that we need to be careful because when you show people your heart, many will capitalize and take full advantage of you. John is teaching them in application, "Stay in the faith and do not be swayed or take part in false teachings." Good counsel for us all! Shortest sermon ever? Nope. Read Jonah's. His was eight words (Jonah 3). Jonah was an angry No. 2 . . . angry, but honest.

Now, back to my internet rant for a moment. It's so easy to catch up with the world around us with the mere push of a button. Fifty years ago, a letter was awesome, and still is! (When is the last time you wrote one?) It's not just something nostalgic; rather, it means someone has taken time out of their schedule to write a note to you and spend fifty-eight cents to mail it. John could have written longer letters, of course. He could have taken more time to write out all the things going on in the ministry and sent those letters on through the Israeli Mail system, where the receiving party—in this case the elect lady and her children—would have received them with joy. But his basic message is brief, urging something that we need greatly to pick up on today: internet-free fellowship.

What a difference this has made in my ministry! I used to constantly tell our youth director that my tombstone one day will read "Unplugged." I know the church staff thought I was nuts (and admittedly I am. You have to be as a No. 2), but the point here is, I have a relationship with people. I've learned what they like, what they hate, what makes them laugh, and how to comfort them when they cry. I know their allergies, where they live, sports favorites or the loathing thereof, and their favorite foods. I spend time with them. As a fellow No. 2, I pray with and for them . . . So did John. He loved people because He wanted to be like Jesus.

In 2 John 12, he's saying, "This letter is unable to satisfy my longing to be with you! We gotta get together!" When was the last time you said that about anyone? It was eating John alive that he couldn't be with those saints at that moment of writing. He knew the joy that would be so wondrously filled upon his arrival, ah, and the first sight when he would see them again as he crested the hill had to have been in his mind and heart.

John hits a key point with what we're on about in this chapter. No amount of social media will ever be able to replace face-to-face fellowship. Remember that. Facebook, Twitter, and the like are great tools, no question! But they will never give the joy of personal fellowship. The same is true of email, Skype, Zoom, FaceTime, Messenger—whatever other means of social communication you use.

At this point, you may be saying, "Great, but what does this have to do with canceling church because there's no internet? What does it have to do with being No. 2? I read the whole chapter, so do I get something free?" Maestro! Next chapter please!

Study Questions

1. What are the advantages/disadvantages of technology and the church?

2. List all the ways that come to mind of how your church utilizes technology. Does it help? Is it distracting in any way (that you feel like confessing in front of everyone)? Does it need improvement? Does it need organization/simplification?

3. Do you consider yourself one who complains a lot? We've observed that by *doing* instead of complaining, one goes a long way to assist in the church's ministry. In what ways are you able to help with your local church or workplace?

4. Do you have joy in fellowshipping with others? If not, what would cause frustrations, or at least the absence of joy?

Personal Reflection(s)

Chapter 3: Mamas, Don't Let Your [No. 2s] Grow Up to Be Cowboys

THE CHAPTER TITLE SPEAKS for itself, I know. However, in order to fill some pages in this book, let me talk about it for a few minutes. Parents want the absolute best for each of their children. There is no question here. They want them to have every good thing their kids desire and need. They want them to make straight A's, ace the state exams, attend the best school for their vocation, have the car, the house and they want their future family to succeed in everything they put their heart and mind to. In other words, we want our children to be No.1s.

Most parents love their children no matter what. They will be proud of them, and as Christian parents, their main desire is to see their kids grow in the Lord and glorify him in their words and actions. So, what happens when through life, you begin to see the child or children you wanted to be a No. 1 become a 2 instead? In some cases, when anything less becomes reality, parents begin to compromise and rationalize, explaining away why their kid didn't win State like their dad did back in the day, or why at thirty-eight they're still unmarried, or . . . you fill in the blank here. What happens when life shows a different path?

We're coming back to the central theme of this book, servanthood, and really getting serious. (I had to lead you along a little so you'd keep reading.) Nobody in their right mind wants to run internet cable. Nobody wants to be the garbageman. Nobody wants to be the person who has to clean up after everybody else. Think about it this way. Think baseball.

I hate the sport of baseball. I want to like it, I really do . . . it's America's pastime! The most beautiful fields and stadiums in sports belong to baseball parks, and the coolest announcers (Bob Uecker is one of my favorite No. 2s) and the athletes who play the game are built like brick outhouses. But when I sit down to watch, I fall asleep. Every. Single. Time. I will admit, I loved the old nineties Atlanta Braves team, but I don't know, maybe I just stopped keeping up with it and fell away. I do go once in a blue moon to a game so I can spend time with family and friends, but my favorite part is strike three, out number three of the final inning, which I know is normally nine.

Baseball parks can cram more people around a field of grass than is believable. *Field of Dreams* wasn't kidding: "If you build it they *will* come." They serve hot dogs, pretzels, drinks of all kinds, peanuts, chips, little bobble head souvenirs—anything you can imagine that a fan of baseball would want to buy is there. Nachos and cheese is my personal favorite. (Go to your fridge and grab something—I'll wait.) Health and vitamins go immediately out the window, and the angelic choir sings hallelujah as a light shines down from heaven when they bring that thousand-calorie tub of awesomeness to seat 44F. "And sir, here is your five-gallon drum of Diet Coke." As we say in East Tennessee, "It don't get no better than that."

The average ballpark today holds roughly forty-thousand people. So, if you have forty-thousand Joshua Lights, you have forty-thousand times the cleanup. I can tell you this: every time I have been to a game, that stadium is like brand new. It's thanks to the No. 2s. Without them, imagine your seat never cleaned. Cleaning crews, janitors and garbage collectors are among the most underpaid, undervalued No. 2s in the world. Tip your waiter/waitress and your janitors. Next time your garbageman picks up your trash, give him a tip, or at least say thank you. Bake him cookies or something—I'm serious. Imagine if they just stopped working. They would say something like, "You know, I'm tired of collecting your trash. I believe we're just going to let it pile up in your yard." Yes, thank them and all your No. 2s. It's the least you can do.

What happens when you the parent begin to see your children excelling in servanthood? Many awesome things. Let them serve and teach them how to do so for the glory of God. Parents, let your kid take you to dinner. It might be McDonald's, because it's what they can afford, but let them. And children, when you're older, love on the ones who raised you. Take them out to eat or even cook a meal for them, often. Did you know that according to recent research, it costs an average of over $200,000 to raise one child? (Kids, I think we owe our parents a little something, huh?)

Don't be a cowboy or cowgirl. Don't buck the system and be your own renegade rebel; be a No. 2! We're running low and are in desperate need of a fill-up. Jesus himself spoke about this two thousand years ago: "Then he said to his disciples, 'The harvest is plentiful, but the *laborers* are few; therefore pray earnestly to the Lord of the harvest to send out *laborers* into his harvest'" (Matt 9:37-38, ESV, emphases mine). The context here is the second reason this book was written. *We need help!* The church is running on fumes. The little help we have doesn't always get it, neither do the No 1s know how to help the No. 2s most of the time. This is all the more reason for more people to become involved in the life and ministry of the church or to volunteer for the jobs nobody wants at their workplace or home. In case it's not obvious, which I'm afraid it isn't, let me explain why more folks aren't stepping up to serve. Some are good reasons, and some are bad.

Have you ever heard someone outright respond, *"I don't want to"* when they're asked to do something in the church? Most will not be this blunt, but as I've said before, no one wants to be nailed down to menial tasks, nor even more so when the task is something they're being asked to do all the time. People love command—they love being in charge; they love chairing a committee or all one hundred church committees. The people under those in charge do not love being yelled at by someone who seems only to complain (oops, I mean advise) about them, and it gets especially ugly when those underlings are volunteering their time and effort! As we've said before, no one by nature wants to be a No. 2. But then no one naturally wants to live like a Christian either. Especially at church. Shoot, it's hard for most people to wake up and get their household ready, whether single or a family, to go to church in the first place. Then after all that commotion in the home, after speeding to get to church on time, you get to attend a service where Pastor _____ or Elder _____ or Deacon _____ or church member _____ is recruiting you for work duty before the service even begins. Woohoo! Where do I sign up? (said no one ever).

Let me be honest for you: it's not fun being targeted like that. I've been around a little while, and I've seen more people of my age group happily leave the fold because of such situations. I've had many conversations with young men and women who felt like from the moment they walked through the church door, they wanted to turn and run the other way because everybody was asking them to do it all. This has got to stop if we're gonna make it. Let's quit greeting our visitors like this: "Good morning! Welcome to church! What is your name? Great! We need someone to help take some chairs from the fellowship hall and put them in the classroom, rebuild the sanctuary's roof, add a Sunday school wing, mop the floor, take out the garbage, and run the sound today, all while balancing on one leg and humming "All for Jesus" (only verses 1, 2, and 4, though). Would you help us out?" I'd be like, "No, I just stopped here this morning 'cause I needed to use your restroom, then I'm on my way. Lord bless and good luck!"

There is another side to this, though, that no one wants to talk about. The church is desperate to find help, just like the visitor is desperate to stay away from helping. I've heard most of the excuses or reasons why people don't become involved, and the biggest one is that they just don't feel welcome and feel they're only a means to an end that never ends.

The danger here is that for some visitors who keep on "visiting," this is a way out of assuming responsibility. They just don't want to commit to any kind of service. Let me confess to you something that may or may not surprise you. I had no desire to preach, and I mean absolutely none. My father was and still is a pastor of a three hundred-member PCA church in Bristol, Tennessee. From a very early age, I've been involved in the ministry of visitation. Dad would take me along to meet with church members and people who had visited the church. They came from all walks of life, everything from farmers to high-end business executives. I watched him give countless hours to the ministry and knew I wanted nothing to do with that. I remember when I was first wrestling with inklings of a possible call to the ministry. I was a senior at Graham Bible College for my second undergrad degree. My determination to have nothing to do with that call remarkably changed into a deep desire to be in the ministry. This came about because of a few mission trips overseas. Without going into a rant, let me suffice it to say this: if the Lord can change a stubborn heart like mine, he can change yours too. Not only did he transform my desire, he also equipped me to become a successful minister. I tried to give as an excuse my aversion to studying the classics and reading in general (I preached a sermon to a congregation confessing my abhorrence of reading and found many others dislike it too. We still need to read, of course, but it helps to be honest). Other excuses were, I didn't have time, other matters needed to be tended to first—you get the drill—but ultimately all the reasons for avoidance ultimately pointed back to the Oscar winner, a lack of desire.

I could really go down a guilt-production road right here but I'm going to refrain from it. I'll say this: the church is always in need of help, and you're a perfect candidate. Bathe your candidacy in constant prayer, even confessing your lack of involvement, and ask God to reveal to you the gift he has given you to serve with, and then to give you the desire to use it for his glory. Watch what he does.

The help we do have doesn't always understand all that needs to happen for the church to continue to operate "business as usual," but neither do the No. 1s know how to help the No. 2s most of the time. That's next, when we come back . . . er, I mean, uh, when you turn the page . . . yeah.

Study Questions

1. Is it wrong for parents to desire and strive for the best for their children? Why or why not?

2. When you think of your children being second place, what comes to mind?

3. For yourself, what do you struggle with the most when you are placed under the authority of someone else?

4. Discuss or think about how you may serve in your local church or community. What is your plan of action?

Personal Reflection(s)

Chapter 4: **When No. 2 Doesn't Understand No. 1 . . .**

LET ME IMMEDIATELY GIVE you the main point of this chapter and then talk about it: No. 2s are not in charge, nor do we have the final word. It's hard to swallow at times, but that's the way it is. There is a reason—and a story that illustrates this truth.

Once upon a time, long ago, there was a man who had everything, and I mean everything. Land, animals, kids, probably a vintage prototype of the first yacht. And he loved the Lord. He was His servant. He sacrificed for his children, saying, "'It may be that my children have sinned, and cursed God in their heart.' Thus Job did continually." Then Satan shows up and has one of those conversations with the Father, who asks him, "From where have you come?" After he answers, God says to him, "Have you considered my servant Job?" Satan lashes out and thinks he can get Job to curse God's face by getting divine approval to test him. Idiot. God allows him to do so with the following exception: "Only against him do not stretch out your hand." So, he leaves God's presence and begins to strike Job's property, children, health, wife, and friends with the worst afflictions possible. This would drive any human alive to the lamentations Job expresses from chapter 2 all the way through 37. His "friends" show up and basically humor him with their "words of comfort." It wasn't the case with Job, but inside, I would have been like, "Really? Thanks . . . #'attaboy." In chapter 38, God answers Job, and at the end gives Job back twice as much as he had before and even allows him to see four generations of his family. The end . . . well, I want to revisit some key points in this story.

First, please consider with me a very important question: namely, who was it who allowed Job to be tested? Here, I have a feeling you're asking, what did Job do to deserve all that? Or, as the saying goes, why do bad things happen to good people? The answer is two-fold. First, as the Bible says, "There is none righteous. No not one." Also, "All we like sheep have gone astray. Each has turned to his own way . . ." We're not "good"; as Christians, we're saved from our sins and given Christ's righteousness, with a desire to follow our King wherever he leads us, but we most certainly continue to sin and need a Savior since "if any man be in Christ he is a new creature." Even more important to the question, who was it who allowed Job to be tested? We know God permitted it. But why did Job need to be put to the test? Because the Lord knew his servant. He knew from before the foundations of the world that Job would not turn from him. Remember what Jesus says in the New Testament? "My sheep know my voice. I know them and they know me . . . Not one will I lose."

Now think of the time that passed between chapters 2 and 37. Even a simple skimming through the chapter and section headings in most Bibles will give you a brief understanding. If, however, you're going through a period of suffering, I encourage you to take time to read the entire book of Job. I can empathize with your pain, I really can. The church also goes through these periods, and if you continue in fellowship with other church members who love the Lord, they'll tell you the same stories. Christians suffer some of the worst, most tremendous blows in life you can imagine. Think of our most recent battles with the Covid-19 pandemic. No one saw it coming. For several months, most church buildings were shut down due to the amount of people attending church services. During the time we most need to be with our church family, the government asked the churches to limit attendance. Now, thankfully, at least in Tennessee, we have been able to return to public worship. We know a refined cure for Covid-19 will come one day, but as we wait, patience gets tested and worry is ever-present. We have already discussed the sufferings of Job. No doubt during his trials, anxiety gnawed at his heart and mind. I would also recommend to you David's soul-stirring prayer of Psalm 69 as a reference for further reading. It's such a refreshment in trial. So is the book of Hosea in his heart's bent on recovering his bride. So is the entire Bible. God speaks through his "living and active" Word. Let it minister to you. Let it change your life.

Countless numbers of people through the ages have been transformed by God's Word. Consider St. Augustine and his monumental *Confessions*. If you've never read it, I urge you to get a copy. Book 9 especially deserves close attention. I won't quote it but basically, Augustine finds himself in a park weeping with great sorrow and pathos (questioning everything). Then he hears children saying and singing in Latin *"Tolle Lege! Tolle Lege!"* With this he stops crying and begins to try and understand what they were on about. He did not know whether it was a new game or a song those little children were singing, but it drove him to the Word of God, from which he had run away all his young adult life. He was converted and immediately told his mother, Monica, who had been a No. 2, praying for him all those years for his salvation. *Tolle Lege* loosely translates, "Take up and read."

OK, back to Job. The amount of time that passed had to have been maddening. Job goes through a season of suffering and comes out in the end receiving double. Is that true for all of us? Listen to this very carefully, and don't label me as a health and wealth guy 'cause I'm not: the answer is a resounding yes. We may receive it here, we may not, but all of us who belong to Christ will definitely receive a reward that far surpasses the riches of this world. We will be with our Father in glory, forever. A former elder is quoted often as saying, "If I got any better, I couldn't stand it." Bingo.

How about another story, yours? What is your story of those times when you didn't understand what was going on or why you were being hammered from seemingly every angle? We can all relate to Job. So, what do we do? Here's the devotional: trust the Lord and continue to be faithful in reading his Word, praying, and serving him with joy and gladness. Pragmatically, this is the best advice I've ever received on the subject of personal trial, and it's something I feel like I need to charge you money for, but you paid for this book so I'll let it pass. Here is the advice: do what's next. This guidance keeps us going when times get tough. And you can be sure that one of the most challenging things to deal with is trying to figure out what to do next. The answer is simple: do what's next. As you brush your teeth, comb your hair, go grocery shopping, do what's next and wait on the Lord. He has promised that "he will never leave you or forsake you."

Look, I'm not saying it's easy to go through painful trials or to minister to others who are suffering. I can tell you countless stories of growing up as a pastor's kid (oldest . . . and meanest), but my most affecting memories are of going with Dad to hospitals, nursing homes, shut-ins (men and women, boys and girls who couldn't leave their homes) that would make you weep. On one day, I would be blessed to encounter some of the nicest, most encouraging things people. But the next day, those same people would be the exact opposite, even downright mean. Of course, with so many of those patients and shut-ins, such factors as medication and dementia affected their personalities. This conduct, sadly, reminds me of what is all too frequently observed in churches and the workplace—gossip, lies, manipulation, backbiting, verbal stoning, and on and on, just as Job experienced these injuries.

One more example and I'll quit harping on this. Saul, whose main purpose before he was converted was to remove the church from the face of the earth, hated Christians. He probably made up a tune every time he was able to rid the world of a few more church-freaks, as I'm sure it's how he thought of us. The words of Acts 22:20 are eerie: "And when the blood of Stephen your witness was being shed, I myself was standing by and approving and watching over the garments of those who killed him." You know what the original language means by "approving"? *Rejoicing. Overcome with joy and gladness.* The same feeling when the Tennessee Vols beat the Crimson Tide of Alabama like a drum (we pray it will happen again in this millennium). Reference Acts 8:1 here also. Saul was overcome with joy that Stephen was being martyred. "Yes! Do it boys! I'll watch your coats. Hoorah!" Acts 9 records his travels to continue his mission of removing the Christian witness on the way to Damascus, but his world is turned upside down when Jesus shows up shining a great light directly on him. Oh man, could Jesus ever have just put his finger on top of Saul's little head and instantly pushed him straight down to the pit itself . . . but he didn't. Read this. We begin with verses 3-9 in Acts 9:

> Now as he went on his way, he approached Damascus, and suddenly a light from heaven shone around him. And falling to the ground, he heard a voice saying to him, "Saul, Saul, why are you persecuting me?" And he said, "Who are you, Lord?" And he said, "I am Jesus, whom you are persecuting. But rise and enter the city, and you will be told what you are to do." The men who were traveling with him stood speechless, hearing the voice but seeing no one. Saul rose from the ground, and although his eyes were opened, he saw nothing. So, they led him by the hand and brought him into Damascus. And for three days he was without sight, and neither ate nor drank.

Doesn't this remind you of the dearly loved hymn, "Amazing Grace"? "I once was lost but now I'm found. 'Twas blind but now I see." Keep reading to learn what happens next in this amazing story:

> Now there was a disciple at Damascus named Ananias. The Lord said to him in a vision, "Ananias." And he said, "Here I am, Lord." And the Lord said to him, "Rise and go to the street called Straight, and at the house of Judas look for a man of Tarsus named Saul, for behold, he is praying, and he has seen in a vision a man named Ananias come in and lay his hands on him so that he might regain his sight." But Ananias answered, "Lord, I have heard from many about this man, how much evil he has done to your saints at Jerusalem. And here he has authority from the chief priests to bind all who call on your name." But the Lord said to him, "Go, for he is a chosen instrument of mine to carry my name before the Gentiles and kings and the children of Israel. For I will show him how much he must suffer for the sake of my name." So Ananias departed and entered the house. And laying his hands on him he said, "Brother Saul, the Lord Jesus who

> appeared to you on the road by which you came has sent
> me so that you may regain your sight and be filled with
> the Holy Spirit." And immediately something like scales
> fell from his eyes, and he regained his sight. Then he rose
> and was baptized; and taking food, he was strengthened.
> For some days he was with the disciples at Damascus.

Upside-down difference. Later on, his name was changed to Paul. I could preach a sermon from this, but now isn't the place or time. Yet as a minister I can't just let it alone either, sorry. So, let me say this about it. Notice that Jesus says Saul was persecuting *him*. You probably caught on immediately what I'm fixing to say, but it took a few readings of this for the light to go on . . . anyways I'm slow like that and hard-headed. I thought, "Wait a minute, I assumed Saul was persecuting believers. Saul learned how to do it, and I mean he had persecution down to an art and a science, then put it into practice. Why is Jesus saying . . . oh yeah, right! Because Christ is the head of his church.

As Scripture records in Colossians 1:16–18:

> For by him all things were created, in heaven and on
> earth, visible and invisible, whether thrones or domin-
> ions or rulers or authorities—all things were created
> through him and for him. And he is before all things, and
> in him all things hold together. And he is the head of the
> body, the church. He is the beginning, the firstborn from
> the dead, that in everything he might be preeminent.

These words were written by Paul, incidentally, who introduces himself often in the New Testament writings by the following phrase, "an Apostle of Christ Jesus . . . "

Fast forward to why I bring up Paul in the first place. He was a No. 2. As Christ's servants, we will undoubtedly suffer. I can think of no other passage in the Bible that gives such a powerful litany of a believer's suffering than what Paul writes in 2 Corinthians 11:23–31:

> Are they servants of Christ? I am a better one—I am
> talking like a madman—with far greater labors, far more
> imprisonments, with countless beatings, and often near

death. Five times I received at the hands of the Jews the forty lashes less one. Three times I was beaten with rods. Once I was stoned. Three times I was shipwrecked; a night and a day I was adrift at sea; on frequent journeys, in danger from rivers, danger from robbers, danger from my own people, danger from Gentiles, danger in the city, danger in the wilderness, danger at sea, danger from false brothers; in toil and hardship, through many a sleepless night, in hunger and thirst, often without food, in cold and exposure. And, apart from other things, there is the daily pressure on me of my anxiety for all the churches. Who is weak, and I am not weak? Who is made to fall, and I am not indignant? If I must boast, I will boast of the things that show my weakness. The God and Father of the Lord Jesus, he who is blessed forever, knows that I am not lying.

When in our trials and suffering, which believe me are guaranteed and certain to escape our understanding, we are nevertheless called to remain faithful because our Lord is faithful. He will continue to lead and guide us as we seek him in all matters in life, even when it doesn't seem like it. In our serving, there will be trials. This is something that can be expected, but do not lose heart!

I'm so proud of you. You have made it through four chapters! Keep reading!

Study Questions

1. What's your understanding of the main point of the book of Job? Can you sympathize with Job in his trials and tribulations? Give some specific examples from the book.

2. Have you ever doubted that God loves you? What gives you hope that he will continue to love you all the days of your life?

3. Do you really believe that God can use anyone? Even you? Think on your past. None of us deserve it. How may your past hinder you from serving?

Personal Reflection(s)

Chapter 5: **Because I Said So**

NOTHING MADE ME MADDER when I was a kid than to hear my parents say a certain gut-wrenching phrase. Parents will get a good laugh out of this, so here goes:

"Dad, can I go spend the night with one of my friends?"

"No."

"Why?!"

"Because I said so." (I can still hear them say that . . . twitch.)

"Mom, can I help you make your lasagna?"

"No."

"Why?!"

You got it (twitch). Their word was *final* regardless of my feelings on the matter. Now don't misunderstand me. I'm so thankful for my parents who raised me in and by the Bible; I'm not even close to being funny here. As for the spending the night conversations, you'll be happy to know I did get to have sleepovers with friends every now and then. But more important, it was a lesson in, "Son, you don't always get to do what you want to do."

As for the lasagna reaction, my dear mother was simply protecting visitors to the manse from food poisoning that might be inflicted because of her seven-year-old son's kindhearted attempts at what is known as cooking *edible* food.

"But Mom, Paul was bitten by a poisonous snake and he lived! It says so in the Bible!"

"The recipe doesn't call for gummy bears or Froot Loops. Sor-ry."

To this day, you don't want me cooking anything . . . let the professionals handle that. It's a fair warning to my future bride if she reads this book, whoever she is. I'm like Charlie Brown in the Thanksgiving Peanuts special: "I make cereal and maybe toast." But now that I'm older, I know when to help and when to step away, for the sake of those who need to remain healthy . . . and alive.

Servanthood. Humility. Now once again we're going to dive deep into what it means to be a No. 2. To avoid doing what we know we should, we can come up with some really grand schemes and plans. We can register all the "what-ifs" and plan accordingly. So did Moses. He had no desire whatsoever to do what God was calling him to do. You might have guessed we're going to look at Exodus 3-4. Turn there as you read these next few paragraphs. Pick up *here* when you're finished reading the passage.

* * * *

Ok, you're back!

"Shoes off, Moses! You're on holy ground. I have heard the desperate cry of my people who are suffering in Egyptian bondage. I'm calling you to go to Pharaoh to deliver them." Then, Moses begins to come down with a case of the "what-ifs": "I'm not a good speaker," "I'm scared," and throughout the rest of chapters 3 and into 4, the Lord lovingly and patiently reminds him that he will be with him. Notice the first couple of words in Exodus 4:18: "Moses went . . ." Don't miss the teaching here—he obeyed. It's so easy to pass that over, but let the truth of it fill your spirit even now as you read. Obedience is such a key role in servanthood and humility. Moses did not want to go at all; he even earnestly asks the Lord to send someone else as we read in this fourth chapter. How tempted we are to simply stand by our wants and "stub up," in some cases to the point of ridiculousness. We immediately retreat to some sort of selfishness, don't we? Heavens, it's so easy. Like we talked about before, who on earth desires to be *that* guy, i.e., the one who obeys even though it goes against his own personal desires? It's a heart issue, which we'll discuss later on. Moses was called, and when God calls, we can't ignore it.

There's another biblical figure who resists, and to the point where it's downright funny. Jonah had no intention of going to Nineveh. God came calling and Jonah said, "Nope! I'm outa' here." So, he flees to Tarshish and rents a ride on Get-Away-Boats-R-Us thinking it's all over. Well, he wasn't too far from being right. God causes a great storm to come up, and the men on board are fighting for their lives. Jonah gives one of those heavy sighs of disappointment and says, "OK! OK. Throw me overboard. This is my fault."

The men reply "Huh? No way bro-Jo. We're not going to have your blood on our hands!" Jonah convinces them that this is the correct thing they must do, and do urgently, and then when he goes overboard, God causes an enormous fish to swallow him. In the belly of that fish, Jonah prays for deliverance, and the God of all the universe causes the fish to spit out Jonah onto the dry land. So, Jonah goes into Nineveh and preaches an eight-word "sermon"— "Yet forty days, and Nineveh shall be overthrown."

And the unbelievable happens. This exceedingly great and wicked city that had been around for a long, long time (mentioned in Genesis 10) repents! Jonah's jaw does one of those cartoon drops to the ground. How thrilled he is at the news! Not. Fact is, he is so overcome with anger that he removes himself from the city and sits on a hill awaiting—probably with crossed arms and a peering look—to see what will become of the city. Rev. Dr. James Kennedy would have pictured the scene and described it this way: "I watched the reprobate become elect before my very eyes." Hard to understand how, when the Ninevites truly turn from their sins, Jonah is furious! Then God, as only he can, gets to the heart of the matter. By the way, for those of you who are pastors, a great sermon title for Jonah 4 is, "It Took a Worm."

"Jonah, do you do well to be angry?" God asks.

Through much reading of this book of the Bible, I've concluded that the point of the fourth chapter is this: we don't get our way sometimes because we have no idea of the back story, God's big story. Folks, it is so easy to pout and insist on our own way. It's incredibly easy to look at a situation with many different heart attitudes, and then justify and plead and do everything else to ensure we get *our* way. God's way is far better. As a No. 2, Jonah was taught that lesson. I'm itching to know more of what happened to him as a result of those series of events in his life. I believe I'll see him in glory one day, and when I do, I'll most definitely want to hear all about it. I like to believe he learned the lesson of God's plan for the Ninevites that he was taught.

Jonah was a No. 2 . . . angry, but honest. Likewise, many others in Scripture and in church history were lowly No. 2s. And so am I, by the grace of God. Servanthood. Humility. The answer to the question, "How then shall we live?" is always answered "Lord, how may I serve you next?"

Study Questions

1. What were some takeaways you got from this chapter?

2. Have you ever run from doing what you knew God was calling you to do? How did it show up in your life? What happened when you finally turned to him?

3. Have you ever asked the Lord for a change of heart and mind? Does it, or did it immediately happen?

Personal Reflection(s)

Chapter 6: **No. 2**

I KNOW WHAT YOU'RE saying at this point: "Joshua, you've made me read five chapters but you've only fed me a morsel of what being a No. 2 is all about. You idiot; get to the point." Here it goes—what does it mean to be a No. 2? (Crowd Noise of Applause.) We made it! We're finally here, so let me get right to it. In the previous chapters, we've hinted at some of the key points, and I believe if you're perceptive, you know some of what I am about to say, and the rest, well, maybe not from this angle. *It means being a servant.* To be a servant, you have to be three things: *humble, available, teachable, and flexible.* You are saying at this point, "Umm, dude, that's four things." I'll quote the movie *Happy Gilmore* here: "Oh good, you can count." And the giant man wearing a gun T-shirt says, "And you can count . . . on me, waiting for you in the parking lot."

Humility. Mac Davis' song, "It's Hard to Be Humble," has this as part of the chorus (I'm not quoting the whole thing): "Oh Lord it's hard to be humble when you're perfect in every way. I can't wait to look in the mirror 'cause I get better looking each day . . ." We'll stop there. Don't google the rest of it either if you don't know the song . . . fair warning. If you remember it, I know you're laughing, so you get my point. Humility! The dictionary defines it as "a modest or low view of one's own importance; humbleness." And life gives us opportunities, like patience, to practice it. You don't have to pray for the opportunities—you have to saturate in prayer your ability not only to see it, but to practice it.

Availability. About two years ago now, I bought what I call a super computer. My super computer hovers and hums in the corner of my office at night, secretly destroying enemies under the cover of night in Gotham (I'm sure of it). It allows me some user time; then when I go to bed, that machine runs the world. Not really. But let me tell you a story of how I got it. When your best friends need help, they call on their No. 2s, meaning they call the people they know are available most of the time to help them, or, they call on those who, in their mind, are too weak and vulnerable to say no, or those who are too stupid to come up with a really good excuse on the spot, lol.

Anyway, I had placed the order for this computer a few weeks before and was expecting its arrival within forty-eight hours. I believe the FBI was watching to ensure it didn't fall into the wrong hands (gulp. Hope they weren't thinking *me!*). I spent over an hour building this tower online with its various interior components.

Just as I'm putting the finishing touches on my computer (what type of tower to house all of the internals in, what sort of memory, etc.), I receive a phone call: "Hey Josh, I need some help moving furniture. The only day I have is Tuesday." (Aargh! Same day as my computer's delivery). "I can't get anyone else; do you think you could help me out?" Oh, let me tell you—I could have made up excuses (I know he's reading this too: he's my best friend). I could have just said no, but like I said, he's my best friend, and you don't turn your friends down, especially your best friend if you want to keep them. In their defense, he and his wife would have rescheduled—no problem—but because I didn't want them inconvenienced, my response was, "Sure. Let's do it." Yes, I missed the delivery date but was able to drive to the shipping office in London, UK (kidding) to pick it up shortly afterwards. Humility to help my friend, availability to swallow my schedule in his time of need, and willingness to do it. OK, so that story probably wasn't life-changing, but it is an example. Here's another:

A corporal was traveling by horseback and came upon a huge log that blocked his way. "Move it!" he commanded his men. They couldn't. No matter how much he insisted that he was the leader and that if they didn't accomplish the task they would be punished, the men simply couldn't move the massive log. The corporal sat on his horse continuing to bark commands, insisting that the log be moved on his order. Then, when one horseman saw that despite their strenuous efforts, the men couldn't clear the path, he asked the corporal, "Sir, why aren't you helping your men?"

The corporal chuckled and remarked, "Because I give the orders. I am the corporal." The rider dismounted and helped the men moved the log. As he got back on his horse, he said quietly to the corporal, "The next time your men need assistance, be sure to send for me." The corporal said, "Who are you?"

"My name is George Washington. I am the commander-in-chief."

No. 2s roll their sleeves up and get in the mud with people. No. 2s sweat with them. They stink with them. They get their high-end clothing covered in dirt and grime because one of their own is sinking. They exchange their hearts and minds in conversations with them. They get to know them and their families and friends. They invest their time in others. They want to see their relationships strengthen and continue. They count others' time as more important than their own. They care. They write cards and put them in the mailbox with an Arnold Palmer stamp. They listen. They are humble.

Teachability. "You can't talk and listen at the same time! If you're talking, you're not listening." I will not mention names here, but if this person reads this book, thank you for not giving up on us five-star hoodlums. Boy, did I want to prove that statement wrong every time I heard it. "I can talk and listen! I'll prove it. Go ahead and speak words, and I'll do what I want and repeat exactly what came out of your mouth to prove I can." Not. The. Point. At. All. Wow, did that lesson take this No. 2 (me) a long time to learn! Be teachable. Listen attentively. Show respect.

Flexibility. I've already kind of hit on this with my super computer story above, but I want to focus on another key aspect of this characteristic of a No. 2: being flexible. You don't have to be an expert at solving whatever problem someone needs help with; you just have to be there to lend a hand. As we've discussed already, the busy schedule is a huge excuse we all give these days as to why we do not or cannot be there, and it's hurting the church. I know we have jobs we can't miss (who wants to get fired?). Or we have family get-togethers that must happen for a number of reasons. Or we plan vacations we've worked hard to make happen. But as a pastor I would say this: if the church is not in your weekly plans, you need to give your schedule to the Lord, watching how he will lead and guide your time. Church is not about just showing up for a worship service once in a while or visiting a couple of times in a row. Be a part of your local church, for we are a people called out of the world and saved by God himself to serve him all the days of our lives by our very lives, and oh the joy that brings! Being Christian means being flexible. Being Christian means being No. 2.

You may not get it at first, but I urge you to begin the practice of regular church attendance and participation. You'll be amazed at how quickly you'll grow spiritually. Not that I'm looking for it, but I bet you'll thank me later. Remember the three characteristics of a No. 2: *humble, available, teachable, and flexible.* There will be a quiz after the next chapter, so remember what you just learned.

Study Questions

1. In your own words, define:

    a. Humble

    b. Available

    c. Teachable

    d. Flexible

2. Are there other words you would use? If so, what are they and why?

3. What are some examples in your life that have made you more aware of what it means to be a No. 2?

Personal Reflection(s)

Chapter 7: **Get in the Mud and Expect to Get Dirty**

NUMBER 2S ROLL THEIR sleeves up, get in the mud, and get to work. In the workplace, at school, at home, in every facet of life, the nitty-gritty *has to be done*. We've already talked about the ballpark and what it takes to keep those places sparkling, but let's take this thought deeper. We all serve in positions of subordination in one relationship or another, be it as an assistant pastor, administrative assistant, student, son or daughter, dog walker, caregiver. If you apply getting in the mud and getting to work to your life now, you'll be greatly rewarded, more than likely only in heaven one day, so do not be disappointed if you don't receive the accolades you wish to receive on earth. You cannot expect things to just happen without effort and even sacrifice. None of us has the power to twitch our nose with the dual xylophone sound like Samantha in the classic TV series, *Bewitched*, and make things instantly appear or be finished (*hint: it will be expected of you unfortunately*), but clearly no one has that kind of power. If we did, we No. 2s would be making several, and I mean *several* dollars. Until they invent something to make things happen in this way, let me offer some insight and encouragement in the following paragraphs.

We take things for granted. Each of us is guilty of this tendency more than we care to admit. We fully expect things will be the exact same tomorrow as they are today. Take a moment and think about everything you're surrounded with. For most, they are things like family, friends, acquaintances, job/ministry, educational opportunities, your home/apartment, your material possessions, your health, that are tremendous blessings. There are so many advantages that, if we're truly honest with ourselves (if you're able to read this book you more than likely have the ability to see and read), we are truly blessed beyond anything we deserve.

Think with me about this as I humbly offer an example from my own life. I have the privilege to serve with a nonprofit organization that's an umbrella for global missions of various kinds of team members. I haven't always viewed my position there as a privilege—it took some work to know it is a privilege; I was a pretty selfish dude growing up. For a while, I just saw that nonprofit as a source of income. Bless them for putting up with me in spite of myself.

The nonprofit I'm talking about is Reformed Evangelistic Fellowship (REF), formerly Presbyterian Evangelistic Fellowship. To explain: the name change better reflects the fact that we have missionaries in multiple reformed denominations now; in fact, REF has missionaries, retired pastors, evangelists, and evangelistic workers in over fifty countries. The main work we do in the office is bookkeeping for each of these team members. We have a network of very generous individuals who give via mail or email to the respective team members through our office. We process the gifts and distribute them to each account. Each and every financial gift must be carefully handled and processed, or it could be entered into the wrong place. This is where our staff comes in, to make sure each gift is entered correctly. Day in and day out, the gifts are individually monitored. I can tell you the process is extremely tedious, and if you're not paying full attention, things can accidently get misplaced. If this should happen, we correct the mistake.

Let me share with you an exclusive opportunity to see how other Christians are faring in their spiritual life: accidently mishandle their hard-earned, God-given money just once or twice. You'll be sputtering in a waterfall of discouragement and guilt, synonymous to that of the power of Niagara Falls. I will not give you the pleasure of learning stories and names, but suffice it to say that I've developed strongly in the areas of patience and listening over the last fifteen years of service with REF because I have to. I am by no means perfect, but I *have to be* the calm to the present storm in their life when a gift is mishandled, no matter how numerically small or great. We're thankful for every penny that comes through the slot, so to speak. But please do not misunderstand me—when a stack of hundreds of checks is waiting on just two people to process them, and one is stuck on the phone for what seems to be just shy of an eternity reassuring the donor that all is calm, bright, and corrected, while the other ten tasks for the day are on pause until all the checks and online gifts are processed, it can put you to the test and leave you wishing for more than twenty-four hours in a day.

The above example reminds us again that being a No 2 means getting in the mud and expecting it to be dirty because it is. This leads into the next chapter. Leaders, the next one's for you.

Study Questions

1. Are you or is someone you know the go-to when things need to be done?

2. Do you pray for them, or if you are the go-to, how do you pray?

3. Do you pray for patience? If not, why not?

Personal Reflection(s)

Chapter 8: **Meet Them Where They Are**

WHEN YOU'RE ALL IN for the Lord, you can expect some amazing surprises to land in your path. Take the disciple Philip, for example. Talk about gung-ho! Let's read together about his unexpected encounter in Acts 8:26-40:

> Now an angel of the Lord said to Philip, "Rise and go toward the south to the road that goes down from Jerusalem to Gaza." This is a desert place. And he rose and went. And there was an Ethiopian, a eunuch, a court official of Candace, queen of the Ethiopians, who was in charge of all her treasure. He had come to Jerusalem to worship and was returning, seated in his chariot, and he was reading the prophet Isaiah. And the Spirit said to Philip, "Go over and join this chariot." So, Philip ran to him and heard him reading Isaiah the prophet and asked, "Do you understand what you are reading?" And he said, "How can I, unless someone guides me?" And he invited Philip to come up and sit with him. Now the passage of the Scripture that he was reading was this: "Like a sheep he was led to the slaughter and like a lamb before its shearer is silent, so he opens not his mouth. In his humiliation justice was denied him. Who can describe his generation? For his life is taken away from the earth." And the eunuch said to Philip, "About whom, I ask you, does the prophet say this, about himself or about someone else?" Then Philip opened his mouth, and beginning with this Scripture he told him the good news about Jesus. And as they were going along the road they came to some water, and the eunuch said, "See, here is water! What prevents me from being baptized?" And he commanded the chariot to stop, and they both went down

into the water, Philip and the eunuch, and he baptized him. And when they came up out of the water, the Spirit of the Lord carried Philip away, and the eunuch saw him no more, and went on his way rejoicing. But Philip found himself at Azotus, and as he passed through he preached the gospel to all the towns until he came to Caesarea.

Notice the beginning action of Philip, "he rose and went," or he obeyed. Then Philip meets the eunuch where he was. *He meets him where he was* and asks the question, "Do you get what you're reading? Does it make sense?" The eunuch, not knowing whether Philip could help or not, states the condition of everyone who is outside of the faith, "How can I, unless someone guides me?" Then Philip continues to be a No. 2 and takes time to go through the Word with this eunuch. Yes, it is certainly true that the Lord had prepared the Ethiopian's heart for this moment, and the Lord had prepared Philip for the moment as well. *Philip was available, he was patient, and he was willing*—willing to spend the necessary time teaching and making sense of the Word to a stranger. Philip met the eunuch where he was.

As the church, we do well to model our outreach after Philip and like him, be intentional evangelists in our witness. We should not shy away from sharing the gospel, but be looking prayerfully and expectantly for opportunities to engage others in spiritual conversation with hopes of leading them to Jesus. Simply leaving a soul to God's sovereignty is what I call arrogant outreach. Yes, he will draw his children to himself, and it is our responsibility to meet them where they are.

In 2004 I was twenty-one years old and scared to death. Evangelist Mark Grasso with REF told me over the phone, "Well Josh, if you're going to be my boss, you're going to be an evangelist. Come to Philadelphia and we'll put you on the street sleepless after some training. Bye-bye." So, I went. Oh, geez, I could tell you the stories of the nights of "what-ifs" or "I don't wannas," but I kept all of that at bay and made the trip to Philly. Those of you reading this who are familiar with the Evangelism Explosion outline will appreciate this story. (For those who've never heard of it, EE, as it's called, is an effective evangelistic tool developed by the late, great pastor and author, Dr. D. James Kennedy). I'll give some background so we can all be on the same understanding level here. So, the Evangelism Explosion outline is Grace, Man, God, Christ, and Faith. During the faith "presentation," you were trained to pull out your car keys and explain a few of your keys and what they unlocked. We did this all week. The basic idea of it is this: if your car key can't open your office door, why do you think anything else will let you into heaven besides trusting in Jesus?

I had the privilege of giving my first gospel presentation to a Haitian supermodel who happened to live in Upper Darby, Pennsylvania. This lady was drop-dead gorgeous. The trainers allowed me to present the faith part of the outline to her probably because I had that creeper stare look—who knows, I don't remember. When I reached for my keys, we noticed a huge metal key ring that she had on her person. Folks, it was chock-full of no less than a hundred keys. We laughed together about them after we told her why we were laughing, and she explained that she ran a cleaning business and that each of the keys were to differing businesses. That told me something: this lady is trustworthy and people depend on her. So, we talked about trust and how we are to put our trust in Jesus alone. Although she did not make a profession, she very politely listened, thanked us all for the time we spent in conversation, and accepted the literature we offered. I hope to see her in heaven one day, trusting that the Lord took the seed we planted and who knows, maybe a Haitian male supermodel led her to Jesus. We met her where she was.

Church, please hear this. Lost people will not normally wander into your congregation. Yes, it happens from time to time, but please don't rely on that for one hundred percent of your outreach. The church is dying because we're scared to death to strike up a conversation with someone we don't know. We're dying because we're shy. We have to go meet people where they are, and we have to open our mouths and say words about Jesus. More than likely the eunuch had no clue who Philip was until Philip met him where *he* was. After the eunuch was converted, notice he went on his way, *rejoicing*. We don't beat them over the head with twelve-gage Bibles—we talk to them, and if necessary, yes, by all means hit them over the head with it.

This is the main thrust of the missionary. And, when serving outside the US, these evangelists meet the native peoples where they are. The stories of their efforts are incredibly inspiring. As a chief operating officer of Reformed Evangelistic Fellowship— which as I've mentioned is a nonprofit evangelistic association— I'm not supposed to have favorites, but let me tell you about two of my favorite missionaries who are not affiliated with REF: Newton and Susan Hamlin. The amount of humility and love for people that exudes from the Hamlins is contagious. I'm afraid if I don't talk about them no one will, so let me mention them, 'cause I love their hearts. Newton and Susan are missionaries with Wycliffe Bible Translators to the Nai people in Papua New Guinea. The couple set out to write a dictionary of their phonetics and give them a written Bible in accordance with their speech and sounds.

Now, if you know anything about theology, not just any word or sound will do to translate the Bible. The Hamlins had to spend time with the Nai people and continue to do so, to ensure they were giving them correct terminologies in their translations. They didn't stop there, but took it one step farther. For those individuals who couldn't read their spoken language, the Hamlins recorded the Bible using a solar-powered audio Bible so they could hear God's Word in their own language. When Newton and Susan present their work to churches, they bring the paper copy of their dictionary. Seeing it and knowing the cost of their long and loving labors will break your heart.

Reader, this is a gift of incalculable worth. I'm eternally grateful for the Hamlins and all the other missionaries who serve Christ fulltime in foreign countries and here at home. As No. 2s, let's follow their example and meet people where they are. Let's also remember to pray for the Lord's constant protection and provision for their needs, and give financially when we can. What better service can we offer as No 2s?

Study Questions

1. Have you ever been able to share your faith with someone else? If so, reflect on the experience. What did it mean to you? What would you do differently today than the first time you shared your faith?

2. What are some of the common reasons individuals are staying outside of the church's fellowship? Give reasons.

3. What are some things you can improve on in your evangelistic efforts to reach more people for Christ and bring them into the church's fold?

4. What gifts has the Lord given you to use in this outreach?

Personal Reflection(s)

Chapter 9: **Iron Bars Do Not A [No. 2] Make**

LEADERS, YOU'VE GOT TO give your No. 2s freedom and time to serve the needs that beg for attention. So, let's look at a No. 2s perspective of that wonderful business term, micromanagement. The dictionary defines it as, "to manage especially with excessive control or attention to details." Some of you are going, "Man, you should write a book on that!" Well, it's not the whole book, but a chapter has been dedicated to this from a guy who doesn't know as much as most, but who's been "under the gun" long enough to write about it (Some of you I know are going, "Is this study over yet so we can eat dessert?"). Almost.

To micromanage is to ensure the things that need to be done are firstly done, and done correctly. There is another business term (acronym) MBWA: Manage by Walking Around. Good leaders have practiced this technique since Noah. Noah had to make sure all the animals were in the ark, that they had proper food, but not (pardon the insight) water because there was *plenty* of it. He also needed to make sure his family was doing well and had everything essential for survival. He needed to manage the ark and make sure there were no leaks (talk about opening the floodgates). He needed to keep things on board calm, cool, and collected. One thing about the ark I've only recently thought of: I bet the smell was out of this world awful. Here's another East Tennessean saying, *Shew*. No thanks, right? Noah had to keep it calm even among the, um, stuff.

Leaders: you of all people are aware of the massive number of things that have to happen for the job/ministry to be completed. No. 2s don't think about what those of you in charge have to put up with or manage—they just think about the task assigned to them.

It's easy for leaders to forget the process of how things get done. I encourage you to take a pause now from reading the rest of this chapter and get out paper and pen or your computer, or whatever you take notes on, and write down all the things you manage. Then think about what it takes to accomplish each task. For that you can thank your No. 2s, the ones serving your needs. Next, evaluate those needs and as well as your wants against the time it takes to complete them. Maybe you need to change the way(s) you handle each. Remember, it takes time, not money, to serve. Money can buy you more help, but make sure you've got the space for additional staff. Set up your workspace in such a way that those you employ are able to manage and serve. This will greatly aid and assist you in the future. If you're a perfectionist or struggle with trust issues, releasing authority and responsibility to others will be difficult because the bottom line is that things will not always be done in the way you think they should, but you can evaluate what is important (needed) and what is current (wanted).

Some people love to have leaders looking over their shoulder to ensure they make no mistakes on any task assigned to them. Others hate it. Some people want to discuss every miniscule detail of their work to make sure every thought is absolutely correct. Others just want to get the job done in peace and quiet and go home. Some people love cats; some wish cats were never created. I love what the senior pastor of Briarwood PCA, Reverend Dr. Harry Reeder III says about cats: "You never see a dog standing next to the witch in Halloween decorations." A man after my own heart. Yes, I know these days that's almost hate speech. You're right. I would say other things about cats, but I am afraid that PETA would come to visit, and there would be anger and rage and hurtful things, and I would be beheaded.

No. 2s want to get it right to make the boss happy. Let's go ahead and admit it. We want security of our job/ministry. We want to know that we will still be employed tomorrow. We want to know that the bills can be paid. We want to know that we can go out to eat every now and then, and not have to penny-pinch for everything. We seek security.

Your No. 2s are going to have ideas also. They're the ones who deal with assigned tasks more than you do. They may not know the big picture, but they do see the nitty-gritty. They know what the mud feels and smells like. Hear them out. They don't constantly need to be put in their place or hovered over while they carry out tasks. Understand this if you want to keep those invaluable No. 2s. Leaders, give your No. 2s room to serve. Let them show you what the Lord will do through them. After all, if they've got their heart right, they're seeking his approval first.

Study Questions

1. Leaders: How are you guilty of micromanagement? Is micro-management all bad?

2. What are some important things leaders must keep in mind?

3. What if a subordinate has a new idea? How should the leader treat it?

4. Is it wrong to want job/ministry security? Why or why not?

Personal Reflection(s)

Chapter 10: **Not My Will, But Your Will Be Done**

As he hung on Calvary's cross, what went through the mind and heart of the One who had spoken the world into being? He knew what he had said to Adam and Eve in the Garden of Eden as recorded in Genesis 3: "Where are you? Who told you that you were naked? Have you eaten of the tree of which I commanded you not to eat? What is this that you have done?" Sacrifice must be made and Jesus was sent to earth, born of a virgin, to pay our sin debt in full. His sacrifice was a must. Without *him,* we have no future. Without God raising him from the tomb three days later, we have no hope.

What went through Christ's mind and heart when the masses came to him wanting him to heal them of their infirmities while countless others mocked, ridiculed, scorned, and beat him, as they sought to catch him off guard or trick him with their deceitful words, and wanted him nothing shy of gone or dead? Hebrews 4:15 reassures us: "For we do not have a high priest who is unable to sympathize with our weaknesses, but one who in every respect has been tempted as we are, yet without sin." Think of that.

Now let's turn the question to ourselves. What goes through our minds and hearts when yet another task is piled up on our already overloaded slate? What goes through us when we get yelled at for a mistake, big or small? What grips us when we fall short? I tell you what goes through me when I'm overloaded by people who may or may not be oblivious to whether they recognize my heavy workload. Sin. This is hard to admit because I am a Christian! What's with that? I really do want to (and strive to) get it, to put his word into practice daily in my life. This means keeping Christ's sacrifice on the cross in front of me, measuring my own thoughts and actions against the terrible price he paid to pardon my sin.

No one will ever be able to fully comprehend the breadth of our Lord's suffering and struggle on that night of nights in the Garden of Gethsemane. There he knelt, the Maker of the world. The One who created everything we know simply by speaking it into being, and now this same voice cries out to his Father in a mode that passion itself can never define as his tears spilled on the very ground he had created. You know the story. Matthew 26:36-39 says,

> Then Jesus went with them to a place called Gethsemane, and he said to his disciples, "Sit here, while I go over there and pray." And taking with him Peter and the two sons of Zebedee, he began to be sorrowful and troubled. Then he said to them, "My soul is very sorrowful, even to death; remain here, and watch with me." And going a little farther he fell on his face and prayed, saying, "My Father, if it be possible, let this cup pass from me; *nevertheless, not as I will, but as you will*" (emphasis mine).

No greater definition of being No. 2 can be given than this passage. By God's grace, we need to mimic this as much as we are able to do so. Let's look at two passages for further study. First, Philippians 2:1–18:

> So if there is any encouragement in Christ, any comfort from love, any participation in the Spirit, any affection and sympathy, complete my joy by being of the same mind, having the same love, being in full accord and of one mind. Do nothing from selfish ambition or conceit, but in humility count others more significant than yourselves. Let each of you look not only to his own interests, but also to the interests of others. Have this mind among yourselves, which is yours in Christ Jesus, who, though he was in the form of God, did not count equality with God a thing to be grasped, but emptied himself, by taking the form of a servant, being born in the likeness of men. And being found in human form,

he humbled himself by becoming obedient to the point
of death, even death on a cross.

And now comes Paul's grand crescendo, followed by instructions
for us as believers:

> Therefore God has highly exalted him and bestowed on
> him the name that is above every name, so that at the
> name of Jesus every knee should bow, in heaven and
> on earth and under the earth, and every tongue confess
> that Jesus Christ is Lord, to the glory of God the Father.
> Therefore, my beloved, as you have always obeyed, so
> now, not only as in my presence but much more in my
> absence, work out your own salvation with fear and
> trembling, for it is God who works in you, both to will
> and to work for his good pleasure. Do all things without
> grumbling or disputing, that you may be blameless and
> innocent, children of God without blemish in the midst
> of a crooked and twisted generation, among whom you
> shine as lights in the world, holding fast to the word of
> life, so that in the day of Christ I may be proud that I did
> not run in vain or labor in vain. Even if I am to be poured
> out as a drink offering upon the sacrificial offering of
> your faith, I am glad and rejoice with you all. Likewise
> you also should be glad and rejoice with me.

To sum up, Paul says to avoid sin and gives practical ways to help
us: don't grumble or be argumentative. Live pure lives, and you
will stand out like bright lights in a crooked, twisted world. Hold
fast to God's life-giving Word.

Secondly, let's look at Romans 7:4–25, where Paul goes into
great detail about the nature of sin and our fallen human condition, but also offers us encouragement to overcome it and live as
spiritual men and women: "Likewise, my brothers, you also have
died to the law through the body of Christ, so that you may belong
to another, to him who has been raised from the dead, in order
that we may bear fruit for God. For while we were living in the
flesh, our sinful passions, aroused by the law, were at work in our
members to bear fruit for death."

Here's the good news: "But now we are released from the law, having died to that which held us captive, so that we serve in the new way of the Spirit and not in the old way of the written code." And here's the brilliant explanation of how sin works:

> What then shall we say? That the law is sin? By no means! Yet if it had not been for the law, I would not have known sin. For I would not have known what it is to covet if the law had not said, "You shall not covet." But sin, seizing an opportunity through the commandment, produced in me all kinds of covetousness. For apart from the law, sin lies dead. I was once alive apart from the law, but when the commandment came, sin came alive and I died. The very commandment that promised life proved to be death to me. For sin, seizing an opportunity through the commandment, deceived me and through it killed me. So the law is holy, and the commandment is holy and righteous and good. Did that which is good, then, bring death to me? By no means! It was sin, producing death in me through what is good, in order that sin might be shown to be sin, and through the commandment might become sinful beyond measure. For we know that the law is spiritual, but I am of the flesh, sold under sin. For I do not understand my own actions.

He nails it here!

> For I do not do what I want, but I do the very thing I hate. Now if I do what I do not want, I agree with the law, that it is good. So now it is no longer I who do it, but sin that dwells within me. For I know that nothing good dwells in me, that is, in my flesh. For I have the desire to do what is right, but not the ability to carry it out. For I do not do the good I want, but the evil I do not want is what I keep on doing. Now if I do what I do not want, it is no longer I who do it, but sin that dwells within me. So I find it to be a law that when I want to do right, evil lies close at hand. For I delight in the law of God, in my inner being, but I see in my members another law waging war against the law of my mind and making me captive to the law of sin that dwells in my members. Wretched

> man that I am! Who will deliver me from this body of
> death? Thanks be to God through Jesus Christ our Lord!
> So then, I myself serve the law of God with my mind,
> but with my flesh I serve the law of sin.

We want to live in victory, but even as Christians we will continue to struggle with sin. Don't let this fact be an excuse (see Rom 6). Maybe our prayer should be what my father has said from the pulpit several times in his sermons delivered over forty years of faithful evangelistic ministry— "Lord, help me not to sin as much."

Study Questions

1. Read Philippians 2:1-18. What stands out to you? How can you tell if you're doing something from selfish ambition or conceit? Can you remember a time when you chose to serve someone else rather than be served yourself? What was the benefit?

2. Read Romans 7:4-25. What stands out to you? How can you serve in "the new way of the Spirit" and not "in the old way of the written code?"

3. Do you consider yourself teachable? Humble? If yes, how are you proving this to be true? If no, what might you do to change that?

4. List some other references that explain how Jesus is able to further make us into servants. What have you learned or been reminded of in studying how our Lord and Savior served the will of God for us?

Personal Reflection(s)

Chapter 11: **So Send I You**

CONGRATULATIONS! YOU ARE NOW armed and ready to be a No. 2 (if you didn't already know that). The title of this chapter is the hymn of the faith we sing every time we have a commissioning service at our Reformed Evangelistic Fellowship Conferences. It's perfect.

Jesus came to this earth, rose from the grave, and just before ascending to the right hand of the Father, he gave his disciples one more lesson. You would think that after all that, they would begin to understand: it's almost like the scene in *The Matrix* where Neo is finally figuring out that he can do some really cool stuff, and then comes that dramatic moment where Morpheus (the guy with the awesome clip-on sunglasses) says of Neo, "He's beginning to believe." You would think! Let's look at Acts 1:6-11:

> So when they had come together, they asked him, "Lord, will you at this time restore the kingdom to Israel?" He said to them, "It is not for you to know times or seasons that the Father has fixed by his own authority. But you will receive power when the Holy Spirit has come upon you, and you will be my witnesses in Jerusalem and in all Judea and Samaria, and to the end of the earth." And when he had said these things, as they were looking on, he was lifted up, and a cloud took him out of their sight. And while they were gazing into heaven as he went, behold, two men stood by them in white robes, and said, "Men of Galilee, why do you stand looking into heaven? This Jesus, who was taken up from you into heaven, will come in the same way as you saw him go into heaven."

After all that, and you can almost see our Lord and Savior do a palm-face—one of those "could've had a V8" disappointed, hand-smack-forehead moments. His attitude was and is infinitely better and different than mine; after all, that's what I would've done. "Guys! Where ya been? Have you not paid attention to anything *that's just happened!* Here's another way of thinking about it that may offend some of you (please don't let it): "Jesus, are you going to Make Israel Great Again?" Perhaps their MIGA hats were blue and not red. Blue like the Star of David. The point is this: Jesus politely answers them and charges all readers to continually put to practice what he says in verses 7-8. In short, your concern is not national restoration, but your responsibility is to witness of Jesus to the world. They did just that. They got it. All served him until their death. That is our charge as well.

This book is centered on the Master No. 2, Jesus Christ. He is the lamp unto our feet and the light unto our path. My prayer for you, reader, is that he continue to shine the way for us to serve him with joy and gladness until the day when he calls us to our eternal home. Another pastor friend of mine, who was my boss for a few years in Johnson City, has concluded a few sermons with this thought: "As Christians, we will hear the Father of all say to us one of two things. The first is what we all want to hear: 'Well done, good and faithful servant. Enter now into the eternal rest prepared for you from before the foundations of the world,' or the second, according to his promise— 'Welcome home.'" No. 2, which one do you want to hear him say to you?

Personal Reflection(s)

Appendix: **Professional Advice from a No. 2**

GOD'S TIME. YOUR TIME. Their time. That's the order. Never forget it and don't let anyone tell you you're sinning because you insist on those priorities. People are professional manipulators and will drive you absolutely crazy if you let them. A pastor friend of mine told a bunch of us when we were wide-eyed in seminary, "Make your schedule, or you *will* be a part of someone else's." Nail that down, I beg you, in your hearts and minds. At first, I know it sounds cold and crass, but the manipulators out there will take phrases from the Word and make up their own meaning from them and run you over with a smile and a purpose of being a part of their agenda. They are good at it and you're not prepared for the onslaught of stuff. Pray that God will take your schedule and that he will reveal himself to you through it that you may serve him to the best of your ability that he will further sanctify in you. And for his sake, please put away the pseudo-guilt those of us feel who are already overloaded with tasks. This is a guilt that constantly hammers at our hearts that says do more. Lord bless you in that, 'cause you'll never feel like you've accomplished anything. Leave it to him. Be a No. 2 in Jesus' name and for his glory. We need you. We really do need you.

Personal Reflection(s)

About the Author

JOSHUA LIGHT IS A native of Tennessee and serves the Reformed Evangelistic Fellowship in Bristol, Tennessee as the chief operating officer. He is also an adjunct professor of missions and evangelism at Graham Bible College. He is a graduate of Northeast State Community College with an associate's degree in philosophy, and earned a bachelor of biblical education from Graham Bible College in 2009. He studied at Birmingham Theological Seminary in 2015, graduating with a master of divinity, and is scheduled to complete a doctorate in ministry degree through the same seminary.